La Tierra en acción/Earth in Action

Terremotos/Earthquakes

por/by Mari Schuh

Editora consultora/Consulting Editor: Gail Saunders-Smith, PhD

Consultora/Consultant: Susan L. Cutter, PhD
Distinguida Profesora y Directora de Carolina/Carolina Distinguished Professor and Director
Instituto de Investigación de Peligros y Vulnerabilidad/Hazards & Vulnerability Research Institute
Departamento de Geografía/Department of Geography
University of South Carolina

CAPSTONE PRESS
a capstone imprint

Pebble Plus is published by Capstone Press,
151 Good Counsel Drive, P.O. Box 669, Mankato, Minnesota 56002.
www.capstonepub.com

Books published by Capstone Press are manufactured with paper containing at least 10 percent post-consumer waste.

Library of Congress Cataloging-in-Publication Data
Schuh, Mari C., 1975–
    [Earthquakes. Spanish & English]
    Terremotos = Earthquakes / por Mari Schuh.
    p. cm.—(Pebble Plus bilingüe. La tierra en acción = Pebble Plus bilingual. Earth in action)
    Summary: "Describes earthquakes, how they occur, and the damage they cause—in both English and Spanish"—Provided by publisher.
    Includes index.
    ISBN 978-1-4296-5358-9 (library binding)
    1. Earthquakes—Juvenile literature. I. Title. II. Title: Earthquakes.
QE521.3.S37818 2011
551.22—dc22   2010004991

Editorial Credits
Erika L. Shores, editor; Strictly Spanish, translation services; Lori Bye, set designer; Wanda Winch, media researcher; Eric Manske and Danielle Ceminsky, designers; Laura Manthe, production specialist

Photo Credits
Alamy/Roy Garner, 5
AP Images/Nick Ut, 21
Compass Point Books/Eric Hoffmann, 7
FEMA News Photo/Robert A. Eplett, 1
Getty Images Inc./AFP/Jes Aznar, 17; AFP/Liu Jin, 13; AFP/Teh Eng Koon, cover; David McNew, 15
Newscom/Kyodo, 19
Peter Arnold/Kevin Schafer, 11
Shutterstock/anthro, 9

Note to Parents and Teachers

The La Tierra en acción/Earth in Action set supports national science standards related to earth science. This book describes and illustrates earthquakes in both English and Spanish. The images support early readers in understanding the text. The repetition of words and phrases helps early readers learn new words. This book also introduces early readers to subject-specific vocabulary words, which are defined in the Glossary section. Early readers may need assistance to read some words and to use the Table of Contents, Glossary, Internet Sites, and Index sections of the book.

Printed in the United States of America in North Mankato, Minnesota.
012011
006069R

Table of Contents

Tabla de contenidos

What Is an Earthquake?

Earthquakes are the sudden movement of the earth's surface. Roads can bend and crack. Buildings can fall.

¿Qué es un terremoto?

Los terremotos son el movimiento repentino de la superficie de la Tierra. Las calles y carreteras pueden doblarse y quebrarse. Los edificios pueden derrumbarse.

How Earthquakes Happen

Earth's surface is called the crust.
Huge pieces of rock make up
the crust. These rocks are
called plates.

Cómo ocurren los terremotos

La superficie de la Tierra se llama
corteza. Piezas enormes de roca
forman la corteza. Estas rocas
se llaman placas.

Earth's Plates/ Placas de la Tierra

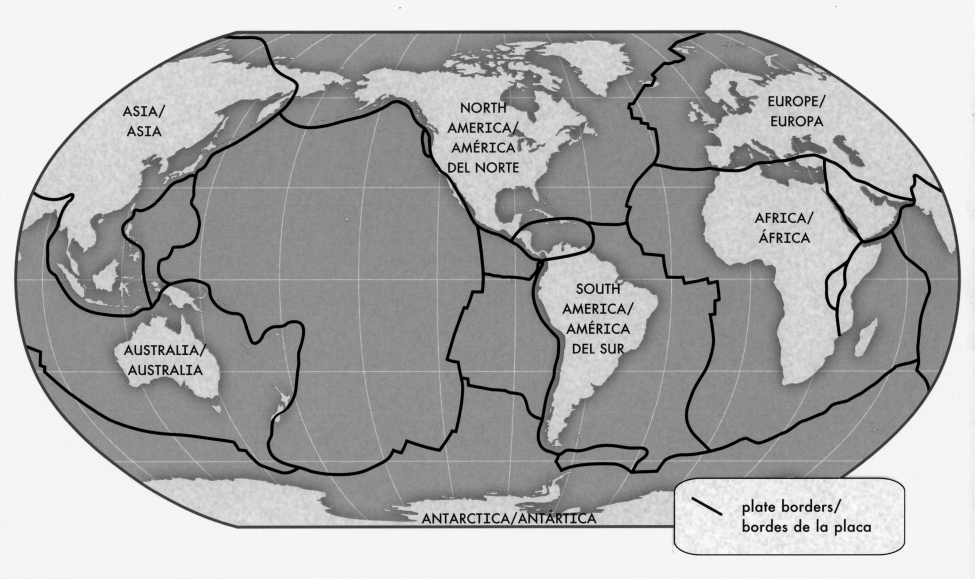

ASIA/
ASIA

NORTH
AMERICA/
AMÉRICA
DEL NORTE

EUROPE/
EUROPA

AFRICA/
ÁFRICA

AUSTRALIA/
AUSTRALIA

SOUTH
AMERICA/
AMÉRICA
DEL SUR

ANTARCTICA/ANTÁRTICA

plate borders/
bordes de la placa

Plates can push against each other. One plate can also move under another. Sudden movement shakes the earth.

Las placas pueden empujarse unas a las otras. Una placa puede también moverse debajo de la otra. Movimientos repentinos hacen que el suelo tiemble.

How Plates Move/
Cómo se mueven las placas

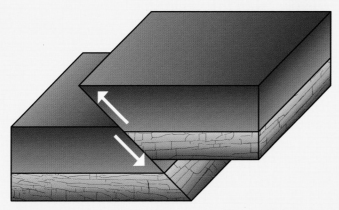

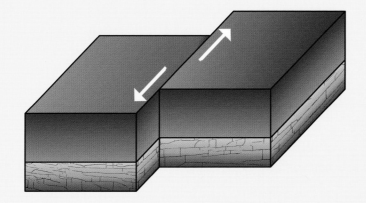

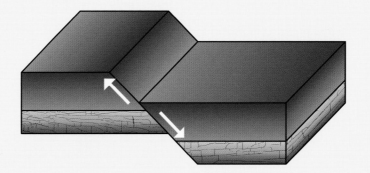

Where Earthquakes Happen

A fault is where the plates meet and rub together. Most earthquakes happen near faults.

Dónde ocurren los terremotos

Una falla es donde las placas se encuentran y hacen fricción. La mayoría de los terremotos ocurre cerca de las fallas.

fault/
falla

11

Staying Safe

Earthquakes happen without warning.

If you are outside, get away

from buildings and trees.

Drop to the ground.

Cómo permanecer seguro

Los terremotos ocurren sin advertencia.

Si estás afuera, aléjate de edificios

y árboles. Tírate al suelo.

13

If you are inside,

move away from windows.

Drop to the floor and

hide under a desk or table.

Si estás adentro,

aléjate de las ventanas.

Tírate al piso y escóndete

debajo de un escritorio o mesa.

Learning about Earthquakes

Scientists use seismographs to measure earthquakes. These machines record how much the earth moves.

Aprende sobre los terremotos

Los científicos usan sismógrafos para medir los terremotos. Estos equipos registran cuánto se mueve el suelo.

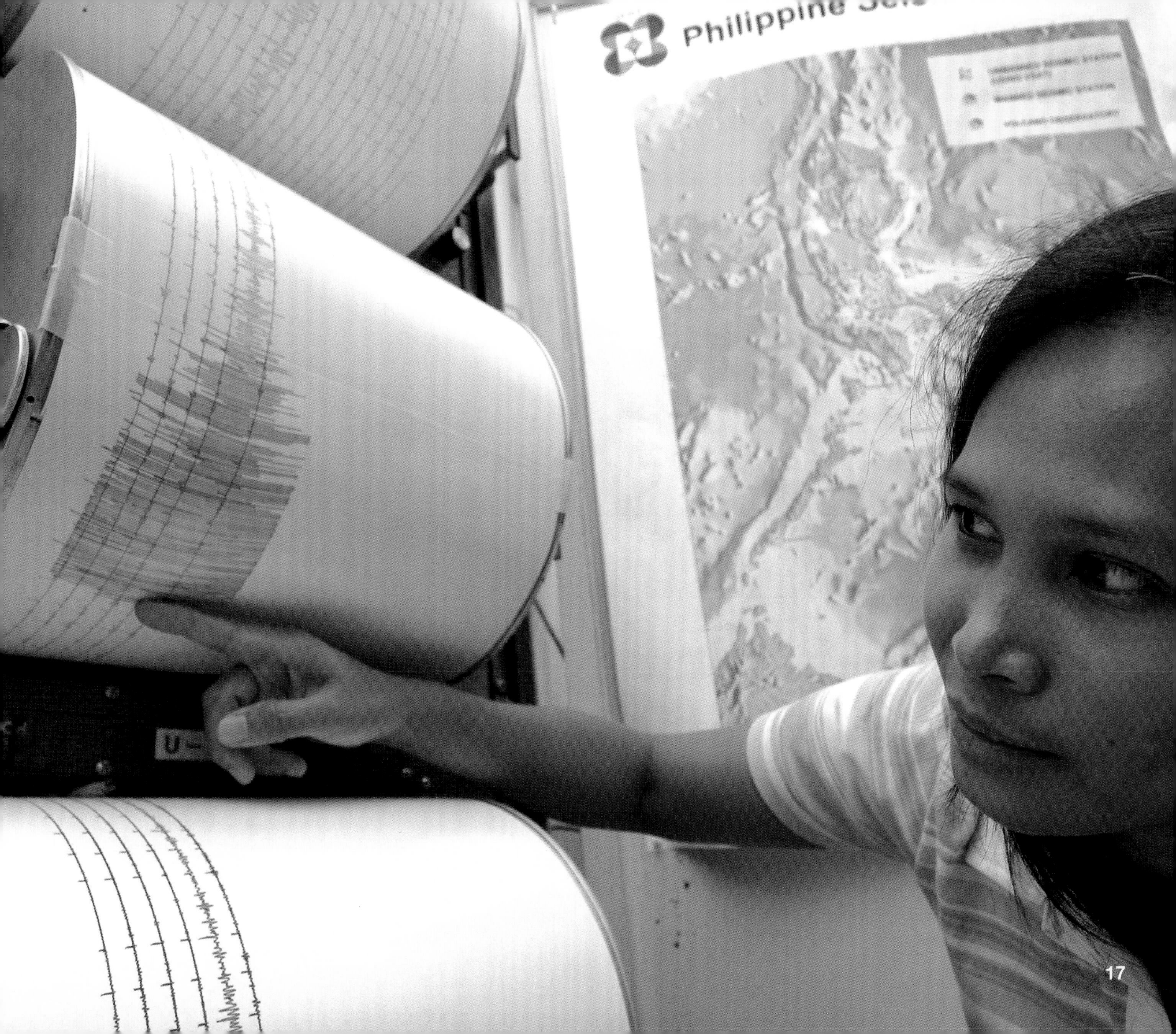
Philippine

Scientists use the Richter scale
to compare earthquakes.
Strong earthquakes measure
6.0 or higher on the scale.

Los científicos usan la escala de
Richter para comparar terremotos.
Los terremotos fuertes miden
6.0 o más en la escala.

19

Builders are making stronger buildings and bridges. People work to keep us safer when the ground shakes.

Los constructores están haciendo edificios y puentes más fuertes.
La gente trabaja para mantenernos seguros cuando el suelo tiembla.

Glossary

crust—the hard outer layer of Earth

fault—a crack in Earth's crust; some faults are just a few inches long; other faults stretch for hundreds of miles

measure—to find out the size or strength of something

plate—a large sheet of rock that is a piece of Earth's crust

Richter scale—a scale that measures the amount of energy in an earthquake; earthquakes with low numbers cause little or no damage

scientist—a person who studies the world around us

seismograph—a machine used to measure earthquakes

Internet Sites

FactHound offers a safe, fun way to find Internet sites related to this book. All of the sites on FactHound have been researched by our staff.

Here's all you do:

Visit *www.facthound.com*

Type in this code: 9781429653589

Glosario

el científico—una persona que estudia el mundo que nos rodea

la corteza—la capa dura más externa del suelo

la escala de Richter—una escala que mide la cantidad de energía en un terremoto; los terremotos con números bajos causan poco o ningún daño

la falla—una quebradura en la corteza del suelo; algunas fallas tienen sólo unas pulgadas de largo; otras fallas se estiran por cientos de millas

medir—calcular el tamaño o fuerza de algo

la placa—una lámina grande de roca que es parte de la corteza de la Tierra

el sismógrafo—un equipo usado para medir terremotos

Sitios de Internet

FactHound brinda una forma segura y divertida de encontrar sitios de Internet relacionados con este libro. Todos los sitios en FactHound han sido investigados por nuestro personal.

Esto es todo lo que tienes que hacer:

Visita *www.facthound.com*

Ingresa este código: 9781429653589

Index

Índice